WHAT BOOKS PRESS

AN IMPRINT OF

THE GLASS TABLE

COLLECTIVE

LOS ANGELES

ALSO BY LAURIE BLAUNER

POETRY

Other Lives
Self-Portrait with an Unwilling Landscape
Children of Gravity
Facing the Facts
All This Could Be Yours
Wrong
Figments (& other occurrences)

FICTION

Somebody
Infinite Kindness
Instructions for Living
The Bohemians

IT LOOKS WORSE THAN I AM

LAURIE BLAUNER

LOS ANGELES

Copyright © 2014 by Laurie Blauner. All rights reserved. Published in the United States by What Books Press, the imprint of the Glass Table Collective, Los Angeles.

Poems in this collection appeared in their present and earlier versions in the following publications: "Time Is Abundant in These Small Spaces" and "It Looks Worse Than It Is" (changed to "It Looks Worse Than I Am") in *basalt*; "The Hand That Feeds" and "What Kind of an Animal Would Do That?" in *Bitter Oleander*; "Hotel Room Interview" in *Clackamas Literary Review*; "In the Room of Another" and "Room for the Storage of Innocent Bystanders" in *Cream City Review*; "A Boy and His Animal" in *Denver Quarterly*; "Be Like the Others" and "Making Its Way" in *Lake Effect*; "Walking the Animal" and "The Animal Who Wasn't There" in *Laurel Review*; "The Keeper of Handkerchiefs" and "Long Ago the Animal Had Too Few Devices" and "Where the Animal Goes I'll Follow" in *Mid-American Review*; "Ordinances for Self-Containment" in *Misfit Magazine*; "The Following Story" in *Mississippi Review 30, 37*; "For Everything That's Contained There's a Reason" in *North American Review*; "The Waiting Room" and "The Living Room" in *The Prose-Poem Project*; "Don't Ask Me" and "Tame" in *Superstition Review*; "Walking Through Walls" in *Talking River Review*; "Excuses," "Containment Training," "Damaged," "Darker Than I Remember," "Last Hours," and "Cannibals Among Us" in *Verse*; "What Kind of an Animal Would Do That?" also appeared in *Verse Daily*.

Thanks to Rich Ives, my husband David Dintenfass, Karen Kevorkian, and everyone at What Books Press.

Publisher's Cataloging-In-Publication Data

Blauner, Laurie.

  It looks worse than I am / Laurie Blauner.

  pages ; cm

  ISBN-13: 978-0-9889248-6-4

  ISBN-10: 0-9889248-6-2

  1. American poetry. I. Title.

PS3552.L3935 I85 2014

811/.54

What Books Press
363 S Topanga Canyon Blvd
Topanga, CA 90290

WHATBOOKSPRESS.COM

Cover art: Gronk, *untitled*, mixed media on paper, 2013
Book design by Ash Goodwin, ashgood.com

IT LOOKS WORSE THAN I AM

CONTENTS

EVOLUTION

That Was Then	12
The Hand That Feeds	13
Dressing the Animal	14
Walking the Animal	15
The Keeper of Handkerchiefs	16
Long Ago the Animal Had Too Few Devices	17
Where the Animal Goes I'll Follow	18
A Boy and His Animal	19
What Kind of an Animal Would Do That?	20
The Animal Who Wasn't There	21
The First Animal to Eat Another Animal	22
The Following Story	23
This Isn't My History	24
There You Are	25
Tame	26

CONTAINMENT

A Fly, Alighting	30
The Living Room	31
Walking Through Walls	32
The Waiting Room	33
Inside I Fall	34
Hotel Room Interview	35
Time Is Abundant in These Small Spaces	37
Interrogation	38
It Looks Worse Than I Am	39
Keep Them In and Then Out	40
For Everything That's Contained There's a Reason	41
In the Middle of It	42
Room for the Storage of Innocent Bystanders	43
Up Against It All	44
Don't Ask Me	45
Entertaining in the Room with All Kinds	46
In the Room of Another	47

RELEASE

Ordinances for Self-Containment 50
Sad Childhood 51
Making Its Way 52
Excuses 53
The Dead Are Disguised by Their Enormous Resilience 54
The Case of the Stuttering Man 55
Be Like the Others 56
Containment Training 57
The Cannibals Next Door 58
Damaged 59
The Others Watch a Movie 60
Skin Lesson with Clouds 61
Self-Help 62
Darker Than I Remember 63
Their Tiny Jars 64
Fragments of the Self-Contained Man's Diary 65
Last Hours 67
Cannibals Among Us 68

EVOLUTION

THAT WAS THEN

When there isn't any fur in its mouth, the animal responds when spoken to. When there are implements for the making of circles and squares, the animal invents trees whose branches point everywhere. The sun is something unfinished and lingering between leaves.

The animal thinks: I should have put my paw down.

A season sleeps against jagged hips and its territory spreads out, humming a vegetative tune. Hanging fruit isn't in the mood yet. The animal juggles the fruit. Adapts.

Where there's friction there can be fire. The animal leans toward the shadows in the heat, waiting for another animal calling, climbing, claiming. The animal doesn't know it's an animal.

THE HAND THAT FEEDS

The animal is ready for anything, variable landscapes, aromas, stretching a paw that's still the same paw. There's blood coursing against human seams right in front of the metal bars.

The animal knows how blood wants to swim free, fill a mouth as sadly as language. There are the old tricks: a ball between some knees; the circle of fire that's hard to miss; a melody that prompts the animal to go to the other side.

A bird in the sky terrifies.

The animal falls away from its own voice, waits for something dead.

Sunrise gathers. The animal doesn't think about how new meat raises the hair along its spine, spills fingers.

DRESSING THE ANIMAL

Everything is done for the animal: water, sky, grass, hats, suits, gloves. It's a show and food is everywhere all at once. Hollow sleeves whisper to a body, any body. Who knows how long this beastly occasion will take, which has nothing to do with the animal. It's times like these when a leg is caught or the hinge of a neck flies off by mistake. The animal can answer that time is definitely not a flowery dress or gleaming jewelry, but the animal can't say what time is, only that it's like a headache that gets better or worse.

All creaturely events are easier for someone else's animal. These things unfold, refold. There's an avalanche of people feeling good about ties and sunglasses. For years trees slowly pushed themselves out of the way. Now they have to be cajoled. Previously, windows could be hazardous, mirrors ridiculous. Now nothing is needed but the latest lunch specials. The animal forgets, runs toward a horizon, whether it's real or not. The animal pants. Its disguise tumbles off; it's happy, rolling around repeatedly. The animal will never understand.

WALKING THE ANIMAL

Half a life away, the animal knows what I couldn't imagine. I can't pretend to be someone else or hide anything. My commands are short and the animal's wild adventures have encyclopedic differences. We meet the animal without eyebrows, the animal that doesn't chew its food, the animal that smells everyone everywhere. The usual suspects. I use big verbs to confuse the animal, but the animal sees right through me, to the nearest hydrant. It's one exciting thing after another. The animal wants an opportunity to make a new life. It wouldn't send me a postcard or apologize. My future would grow unpredictable and tame. All my imagined parts would be lost. I'd learn how to lie comfortably.

THE KEEPER OF HANDKERCHIEFS

There's no place left for the animal to be an animal. Shimmering objects, piles, the dream of what can be done so the animal can rest. Trees are deranged, bushes tangled by steel and glass, cement goes on and on and never seems to let go. Everything will be replaced. Where is grass hidden? The energetic flowers? Zigzagging insects? The windows and windows and windows keep on appearing in front of the animal's face. All the better to break a neck. That's why open doorways and fluttering linen are impossible to resist. The animal is dizzy with choices and an almost empty sky. It listens for the songs of like animals. It notices something large and clumsy watching it from inside while doing laundry. And the very thing it wants falls to the ground, pleading to be plucked.

LONG AGO THE ANIMAL HAD TOO FEW DEVICES

Once the animal was wild about everything. It roamed the periphery of its world with its ornamental skull, playful heart, large, lacerated body, hollow from the get-go. Sun was caught in the animal's teeth. The unsteady beauty of stones rattled its cage. It wandered. Even monkeys needed more than the animal could offer. There was mating, food, sometimes warmth. The animal was awkward when asked. Leaves were born ragged, bones discarded, the lake was the moon's toy. There were too many places to go. The animal had to watch for any little movement. Mice and birds were small, rhetorical. While biting some brontosaurus's extraordinary neck the animal wondered if the problems were all in its head. Looking closer, they weren't.

WHERE THE ANIMAL GOES I'LL FOLLOW

The animal isn't bored, exactly. The animal is at the center of a moment it calls extinction, Peaceable Kingdom, or hibernation. A moment of gathering fat, winter climates, howling dreams, which make it twitch the way drinking cold water does. The animal is surprised by the future like someone tapping it on a hind leg. But the animal heeds only itself. For a long time it considered the clouds something to eat. But the animal has left behind bones, a bed of lost twigs, a square and shiny object, an empty bottle. Something will happen, eventually, when sunlight pushes past the mouth of the cave to repeat itself over and over. Now the animal grunts, with its eyes closed, knows what's missing. The animal comprehends love if love is knowing what you need.

A BOY AND HIS ANIMAL

The animal doesn't like water. The boy tells his animal how the lake's surface is a window that trees open and peek through. The moon hates its reflection, and fish remind the boy of what he does sometimes with his face. The boy throws rocks through the near waves and the animal runs in circles, accounting for each splash that wasn't retrieved. The boy mutters that the animal doesn't give him the right kind of obedience or love. The animal likes following something, so it follows the boy to the place where water flattens into sand. The boy always goes someplace that's too far.

The boy doesn't want to grow up. The boy barks and says that he doesn't mean anything by it. He throws a stick that sinks into the water and the boy laughs at the cowering animal. Trees are walking to the lake and bending down. The boy goes into the water halfway and says, *See,* to the animal that nervously nibbles on stubby grass. And then, *Watch,* as the boy swims far out and dips his whole wet body beneath the surface.

The animal smells nothing after the boy flaps a little and then is gone. Everything is quiet except for the birds. The animal whimpers into the evening, leaves to find a new boy.

WHAT KIND OF AN ANIMAL WOULD DO THAT?

There's blood everywhere and a throat full of rabbits. Intent is what happens to others. There's a still life with everything but the animal: a collar of rain; the necessary fences and houses; hands that unlock doors; feet that try to keep anything useful or delicious away. The world is raw and you can't see the animal coming.

The animal sifts through its instincts to find just the right one. The animal believes in itself, a fur of feeling rising against its teeth, obstacles to overcome, sky opening up a field with something of interest. Nothing can be ignored, not an afternoon that doesn't know where it is or crows showing concern. The animal hears the music of other animals, smells something small and soft falling. It can't resist and the animal is grasped suddenly by what hurts it. It can't be saved. Air abandons the animal. Trees pass by and the last human voices are congratulating one another. Somebody's yard fills with a breeze. As soon as the animal dies, another one takes its place.

THE ANIMAL WHO WASN'T THERE

Hours are misplaced and still the world needs an audience. One by one, the animals disappear every day, taking their point of view with them. Spring was nice this year but clouds fell apart, water trying to get to the bottom of the problem. Birds stand by, bees are anxious and murmur about what to make of everything. Wolves pace and yelp with anticipation. Who's next? The throat of a remaining body swallows. What to do about the missing? Something's gone terribly wrong and I pretend to be another kind of animal, one that lives off the fear in your eyes. You think it's all luck, wandering around, pirating and pillaging, the best of the best. I disagree. There's the rumor of an island that no one can reach where the extinct, lost, and discarded animals gather and are waiting. For what?

THE FIRST ANIMAL
TO EAT ANOTHER ANIMAL

A bird describes a distant scene, the deer falls apart, the squirrel goes experimental, a snake gets technical with a shrubby tree. That morning catastrophe wakes up the animal living among other animals. The animal thinks of the beautiful garden it once occupied, a squatter among so many. Those trees blew about, staring happily at the sky; far mountains bubbled effortlessly. Everything the animal touched was green. The animal asked too much, pretending to be what it wasn't. The animal was wrong. All the other animals tried to read the animal, translating.

Who remembers that old static sky? Mountains and grass change constantly now. You can't tell another animal anything.

THE FOLLOWING STORY

First there were the animals. They were like glimpses of people we might have loved, with no known addresses or names to be manhandled. Everything was left to itself. All day there were experiences and acts.

One day a voice rose like a coin passed back and forth. Animals began to juggle food in the middle of our new streets. We pretended we knew where to go, the houses, fences, and backyards that we might have deserved.

Always, that stray that followed us, wondering about something better over there, and, *oops*. The end of one story, the beginning of another. It resulted in our being alone, breathing audibly in small rooms where the sun winked through a brow of trees.

We loved our memories of animals.

Then one of us invented a way to bring the far hills and green mountains inside. We stepped into any room and something bloomed, a mistake because soon none of us were left.

All the animals returned.

THIS ISN'T MY HISTORY

One forgets things, searches for another town, not remembering the bargains that were made. The newest animal is always thinking about tomorrow and more to acquire. The animal wants progress, but it holds the shrinking houses awfully close. If these things are pointed out, the other animals begin migrating. They wish to start over again. History stumbles into the light and falls back, startled.

There are so many things to consider when the animal leaves, fruit-colored flowers or the commotion of a highway, questions that don't approach. Everything is afterwards. The town remembers the animal another way, molting, large, a special animal that did lovely things.

The town's not holding its breath and wants any animal who understands its streets and trees.

Trees with fingers of color attract a certain kind of animal.

The town accuses the animal of something it can't remember. The animal moves on.

The town is left staring at abandoned photographs, coins, balls, maps, pieces of toys until everyone forgets who owned them.

THERE YOU ARE

The animal is mine for a moment. Behind the wall I imagine fur and a pause before pouncing. Our eyes locked. Let me guess what pours out, what's already been done. I feel the sizzle. The animal's body all curves and claws. Feeding time wasn't always someplace I wanted to be. Sun over the fake, dirty stream. People always leaving. All kinds are here, the exotics, the rare, the dwindling, the ordinary.

I would have to break in during darkness since I count too many of me. The animal is calling. Maybe there's love, fluid as water, maybe not. I'm afraid of one movement. There are places I can be while the animal fills. I want to touch more than air. We stare at each other. Suddenly I'm running away from this intimacy and for that I'll always apologize.

TAME

No response and the world became more world. The animal slept in leaves, a noisy weight, pieces from an occasional sky.

I went to hold the animal and its surprise teeth. There was an introduction, guesses, jargon. Fur in my face and I wanted to offer a piece of my hand. Claws and I delivered my testimony. My human part began its own devices:

I told the animal that one from the herd is sacrificed to save the others.
(The animal fed on a figment of bird.)

I explained how to forget.
(Stars salted our skin every night.)

I told a story about water's disobedience.
(And the animal knew it could make me do whatever it wanted.)

CONTAINMENT

A FLY, ALIGHTING

I'm making a small, black cloud in a golden heaven. Air chews on itself inside this museum. I buzz the woman in a red dress, the landscape with tall houses and clouds gathering like hats, the static still lives. Nothing moves but dust. What could I do except bang against here and there? Entrances surround me but exits remain elusive. A tiny light enters and night is fraying. I change this painting and that sketch by moving my thorax, by the placement of my abdomen, my head. Somewhere the scent of blossoms, a conversation, a moon. My wings feel uncertain, weighted down. I need to be pried from vision. I'm embedded in a dazzling gold, compounded in my eyes. A multitude. What good is another body that no one can use?

THE LIVING ROOM

The dead fall over one another trying to get through the door. The light is bright and blue and everyone seems beautiful and animated. The dead wonder whether the girl with the casserole face or the boy who loves forgotten books should be here. The dead remember something that now seems hollow, and they regret hitting the neighbor's dog with their gray car. They want to be good but no one listens. One of the dead stands on the cliff of the others to be able to see the walls, the floor, the ceiling, and windows. The dead rearrange their old furniture. Then they begin knocking and knocking.

WALKING THROUGH WALLS

My former body unlocks in all that ghostly space, room after room, secrets laid bare one after another. My ribcage slides backwards, arms and legs lengthening to nothing. My head flies off into God-Knows-Where as if it's leaving everything behind. Once there was a life, a place for me. Now I can't hold it together. I can't remember why I wanted to hear that music so badly, but I did, bottomless country songs collecting on an abandoned body. *Baby, Baby,* a window says. It knows me. I put my hand through glass, sky whispering and encouraging. I want to reach through a mouth, discover what makes it smile or sing. I'm becoming a photograph waiting for the right spot, a trick of gravity.

THE WAITING ROOM

When could I give you enough? When scars were erased like clouds or my hands grew delusional? I was on a long, theatrical flight when you made me do what you wanted. I'm not myself today. No one medical knows what to do with me. I imitate the missing and for hours sort through magazines. I peer out the window for details. Coffee appears. I look to the sky but it's become little pieces of blue paper in the distance. My headache returns, dragging along the missing scenery. I list all the mistakes, like wearing little red slippers, or too much water in my nose. Soon you'll tear apart all the small, soft things inside me, looking for what? I was the last one to stay.

INSIDE I FALL

I was dissolved in the tiptoe room. Middle-aged, I didn't want to be alone, abandoned, or uncertain as a jar of spilled coins, so I stroked the bassoon bed. I searched in the unmade blankets, tangled sheets, shivering pillows after all the unbelievable tricks were finished.

A long time ago I started in that room. A tightrope stretched from wall to wall, waiting for me to begin. I practiced my introduction. I wanted a little bit of everything, some sequins, feathers, acrobatic skills, a knife between my teeth.

I heard television-like applause among the jeering and thought of a strange, blue-costumed person reaching for a toehold before the room grew empty.

HOTEL ROOM INTERVIEW

Q: Have you been welcomed here?

A: I found some lost flowers, vegetables, and underwear. I get along with the upholstery. The window is arrogant, trying to leave the same way it came in, and the bed is deeply religious.

Q: How can you be so much like me and yet like everyone else?

A: I fill again and again. I have an imaginary door.

Q: Where would you like to go?

A: To meet in predetermined places. There are rules and I have questions.

Q: Can you describe the outside?

A: Everything I'm not: someone's dream of arrival that has departed.

Q: What keeps you going?

A: I rearrange the curtains and sheets every day. I wait for her to return her body to the space that misses her.

Q: How do you feel about glass?

A: It stops me. I see the personality of clouds and nothing comes out of them except rain or an occasional plane.

Q: What disturbs you about the sky?

A: It bothers sleeping vagrants, moving their walls around.

Q: What are your conclusions?

A: I'm watching a sleeping man's mouth break open. I'm watching a humorless woman give up her night. I remove them all in their own time and yet I'm always full.

TIME IS ABUNDANT IN THESE SMALL SPACES

1 Cell 112
He turns and turns like all the men before me, a ceremony. Absence is tattooed everywhere, on shoulders, legs, in the crooks of elbows. I follow a guard when there's a warning bell. I find a yelping bed, a toilet full of the wrong colors. Danger gallops through the corridors, bangs on the bars, eats huge, starchy meals at dinnertime. I want to talk about what I did, the fresh fruit of a body, the inevitable chase, honor seeping away to nothing.

2 Half and Half
I'm transported and I hardly notice the change. The green buttons have small, instantaneous rebellions. The numbers blink. I have nothing to give a new floor but I go anyway. It stops. Only our faces slide open. Even the curves of our mouths are stuck. Our shoes shuffle against one another. These thin walls have stopped hurtling through air and we're all between destiny and the place we left. One of us cries, another beats his fist against steel, another pretends to sleep. I close my eyes and imagine being stranded on a desert island, alone, with all that impossible water and sky.

INTERROGATION

The enormous void in the room won't let me forget the questions. I go to its precipice and fall in. They close the window, tell me stories, show me photographs of a family on vacation. The children are singing and then they are crumpled paper. Did they like their trip? I ignore the hand against my cheek, believing that there are rules.

    —Don't explain.
    —Don't remind them that you're still here.
    —Contemplate shoes.
    —Don't imagine being inside them.
    —Ignore the smell of metal.
    —Think of the sounds as a missing symphony.
    —Don't cry.

Chairs squeak. A desk moves. Light hisses against my available cheek, describing its familial love. I tell them I don't know anything. The loud people who come and go are brimming with techniques to take me apart. Some versions lapse into pain. Others murmur behind my back. No one remembers how to put me back together. I'm thinner. My answers prove nothing. I can fit through a paper slot, except there is no paper slot.

IT LOOKS WORSE THAN I AM

I'm one-sided and condemned. Someone is lying limply in the bedroom, but the light inside is gone. The windows have come together as though praying and two doors are skinned, brown, collapsing like dresses empty of people. The forlorn find me and grow more idle, their mouths slackening. I'm complicated by scars, body against body. I do well for unbeing, for creaking every time the wind blows through. I echo. I have no more glass to offer on a brilliant morning and I try to smile, the same way a person with bruises might.

KEEP THEM IN AND THEN OUT

When I'm lifted, all that's left is folded and hung. Arms and legs have their personal episodes, turned inside and out. All the shapes are tired like scarecrows. I reach for one every day. Surfaces grow thin, then thinner at the slightest disturbance. The hidden, when let loose, say too much. The noise is someone I imagine. I dream of blankets, umbrellas, hats, and belts on boats, in corners, riding in cars. I want to scare impersonal surfaces into making the right choices.

Look, I say, *what we're up against. Everything.* I have seen bones pressed against their skin. I have seen the hidden smiles. I hear what they do. I wish they would keep their choices to themselves, but this house holds up the sky and stops the rain from entering. I can only see what's right in front of me.

FOR EVERYTHING THAT'S CONTAINED THERE'S A REASON

Gravity keeps me in the basement. Upstairs, my mother fingers her scars while listening to the radio. Matches twitch by her side. Father's been burned twice already. My hands move cautiously to Spin the Bottle. The glass is warm and congregates in corners. A line is the distance between two private points. I'm playing myself. Things spew from my mouth and no one hears them. I lift the bottle but it's too sticky and sweet. If our house is destroyed by fire, will it resemble pieces of paper blowing in a breeze?

The episodes in the basement make me think of blue sky. We are surrounded by walls that reflect everything. All places are incendiary. I pull my skin over the sticks of my bones back and forth as though I could begin a flame. Father's gone and my mother closes her eyes, pretending she's somewhere glamorous. I lie awake nights, knowing I need to do something about that ordinary fire.

IN THE MIDDLE OF IT

It takes work, this play. Under glass, white tops spin, lights flare, the ringing and whistling hardly stops. His blood boils, watching the shiny blur of machinery. The score's everything. Silver dolls swirl, making a fearsome noise, and in a painted corner everything else is still happening.

Steel balls blind him as they pour back and forth like water. He knows he's hollow and that the wrong sound can veer anywhere. His twisted mouth is in the mirrors and there are waves of faces down the line. Every machine in the room is bucking, doing flip-flops. He consoles himself with the storm. First one, then one more. He has already forgotten his body. At the tally he can't tell the difference in decibels between metal and his heart.

ROOM FOR THE STORAGE OF INNOCENT BYSTANDERS

My house is unnerved. I used to carry it inside with its bread and water and lonely furniture, until I picked a place with a cement hide and iron teeth, having seen too much. I didn't do it. I never did. Neither did anyone else here. I saw someone unlock his body, someone I knew. I fell apart and then I was carried away.

Outside is small and unmentionable: the air twists with regrets like fur. But I have enough here - my mouth opening wider and wider, my tiny arm hairs stirred into action. I told them that I couldn't hurt a fly. Now flies swarm all around me.

UP AGAINST IT ALL

Tall weeds and overgrown bushes repeat themselves. A body can only stand so much ransacking. An abandoned house grows, sliding into obscurity. I assume and I assume. Earth presses tightly beneath. When I don't sleep, I feel dark waves that leave paradoxes. Explanations flood me: why there's so much dust; how far I fall from what I want; my inclination toward the balcony. My ideas keep their distance, argue. My mind renounces hollow conversations. I can't walk away. It could be my best moment. A girl, the shape of a house, sleeps outside, brushes decrepit plants away. Something leaves my mouth and scrambles onto the furniture. Something is spoken back that says it wants to bring the whole rest of the world inside.

DON'T ASK ME

I find another and teeter over the dance floor. Strangers, with wet hands and bodies that take short cuts, are borrowed, and reflected in mirrors. I snag a sleeve, confess red lipstick on a starched shirt. There isn't much to discover in these entanglements except that feet keep on moving. Our effort is covered with a music that drifts and then begins to whisper. *Keep your head up,* rings out. A flock of birds only suggests a direction. Our hands stretch, no ends to speak of, mismatched. *Higher on your toes.* I tilt, even though he has the better legs. I get lost in repetition and recognition. I lose my way. He gloves my hand, my eye checks the distance between us. *Step closer.* We are all made of such small parts.

ENTERTAINING IN THE ROOM WITH ALL KINDS

I couldn't believe what flapped by, attached to a guest. Once this had been a room for the blind, who couldn't understand periphery. I spread out my hands, felt for misplaced objects. A story disguised as a joke crossed the wooden floor. A conversation lay down. I was out of breath. A wall bared itself, prayed for a concoction of air. Kisses flew by on tiny wings like exclamation points. The shape of things resembled various cocktails, Yellow Bird, Flying Fortress, Golden Dream, Something Blue, Angel's Delight. There wasn't any room for me. Not with the apologetic umbrellas and thick, puddling coats spread everywhere. I told everyone I was here first.

IN THE ROOM OF ANOTHER

1

A girl and I were working closely together. Her body became consequential and the room grew smaller like leftovers. There was hardly any furniture so I didn't know how to behave. One night the moon entered and I tried to sit on it.

Less is more, she insisted.

I'm just waiting for instructions, I told her. We both grew quiet for a long time.

Thanks for thinking of me, she replied.

But I was thinking of someone else at the strange window and the odd door.

2

Her body's organisms reminded me of her room, ticking without sound, surfaces too far from their interiors, something on her face like rain.

I'm counting silences, she said.

I'm not sure what to want. I looked through all that air and saw her unfamiliar ceiling.

We're looking for ourselves, aren't we?

I told her I wanted to live in a foreign country but I couldn't describe it.

RELEASE

ORDINANCES FOR SELF-CONTAINMENT

Be your own god of transparent things.
Leave socks and shoes lined up by size.
Swallow time. Swallow place. Swallow a ritual each day.
Live in a country full of new faces and birds scattering leaves.

It takes a long time to get to the bones but it's worth it.
Ghosts will get your attention, but when you turn, they lose you.
Talk about the consequences.

Death is invisible. Look through it.
Let others see your hands, and theirs, holding nothing.
Your house keeps secrets at night when people are dreaming.

A body slips into its pieces. Sing until undone.
If you stand too close to the meat store you'll be detected.
Darkness covers everything like thoughts.

Lie down with someone, make necklaces, bracelets, belts from bones.
Give each part a new name. Be afraid of the barely breathing.

Answer the continuously bleeding.

Your house has little to say about you and there's no scenery.

There's nothing more you need here.

SAD CHILDHOOD

What could I do with sparkles before my eyes but eat them? I was hungry for a perpetual feast, arms, legs, toes, a nose. I was a brother and behind us wounded women stood in the waving grass. Too many wives fell awake, ran, their scars spreading out into personal oceans. The sky turned black. The whole village was hurt by the hours and men ran through the woods, following trails of blood. They hardly noticed us. My world was water and bread and family. It was the pierced heavens, hard earth, a moon winking between trees. We stood and stood. Animals came near, noting one thing or another. I grew inward. I kept on moving. The stars kept me alive at first. Rain arrived to meet someone already gone so it kept on returning and asking.

MAKING ITS WAY

The Self-Contained Man ate someone he shouldn't have. His body was unhappy. He wandered through a grocery touching everything in the aisles, ambivalent about pumpkins, eggs, candy in the shape of small toes. His heart clutched at his stringy throat. The world was full of signs, apparitions, a girl with braids that reached through his forehead and yanked his eyebrows. He was writhing on the floor. His lips beat backwards. She laughed, pinched his nose. She didn't know what to do with her knees so they folded inside him. He couldn't admit to anything. They wrestled. Peaches and tomatoes fell onto his body. He remembered an old monster movie where a doctor played with lightning and someone came back to life. He wondered if he could return her.

EXCUSES

The man couldn't get out of himself. A clock crooned and strangers' hands reached for him. There was an incision and haphazard arteries picked like fruit. His heart was drowning. He needed a variable wife. What couldn't the body do?

The man wrote, *I wanted a pickpocket, a girl with tricks.* (Later he could compromise.)

A girl he knew always fell during the Dance to the Sun. Light appeared through her membranes. The girl split an organ inside, folded it, set it aside.

A clock breathed into his hands. The man didn't want to run after the clock to argue, so he poked the nameless girl in acceptance and time came out of her mouth anyway.

THE DEAD ARE DISGUISED BY THEIR ENORMOUS RESILIENCE

The man couldn't help the birds that couldn't help themselves, little knuckles that arrived in the great rain, rapping on the village doors. A person could only admit so much. His brain removed as his listless sister was led out. Small, delightful events followed, a celebration with fires, dancing and singing into the night. The birds' chests wheezed and wheezed, beaks leaving nothing, accidents unfinished.

His sister disappeared without a word. He'd fled from her childhood, passed by her, calling her by other names. What could they do with their hunger for one another and all the terrible jokes? They were turning into one another.

Feathers stitched along their eyes. Before there had been sacrifices. Now distance and people in boats remained along the river, circling around him like birds. He was far enough away so he couldn't hear anyone fall. He closed his eyes, already covered with wings.

THE CASE OF THE STUTTERING MAN

The village ate blurred agreements and arguments as though too many people were fighting for one body. We uncovered the beauty of a red moon at night in June. We grew tired of repetitions, limbs flailing, gathering words. Maybe a god was there. Truth leaned closer, toward water gathering the nearby trees.

Women called him a box of surprises when he uttered demands of the sky. Clouds came down and struck him into day. He had failed his ancestors, his body abandoned. He stated and stated. Everyone lay down where they had spoken, except for the Stuttering Man. We had always known language couldn't save anyone, including him.

BE LIKE THE OTHERS

Meat is everyone. Except with a name like Too-Far-Away or Nobody-Special. The ancestors created beauty from bones on doorsteps, skin was parchment for another story, the musical sound of fingernails. Dancing during cannibal time, the man tried to dislodge the people inside, waiting to breathe the archaic air.

They asked too much. Tomorrow's episode could happen too soon. History was stubborn and people repeated themselves. But wasn't he made of the missing? When he sang someone else's song the others rose, unstoppable, like a drink filling a glass. *Be a different story,* they said. *Be what is picked from between a woman's teeth.*

CONTAINMENT TRAINING

1 Theory
Have I taken too much? What parts of you did I like best? Come closer, Samara. There's a man sleepwalking, his end justifying his means. He dissolves before you. That man is full of intentions like ice melting underneath leaves. Show me. Come alive. Let us pass through one another, running across that ice. I remember our ghosts kissing in front of a predictable fire. I remember our ghosts floating, growing smaller even as we reached toward a surface of light.

2 Practice
I'm tired of tourists and their pretty limbs. I'm tired of the decorative windows and rooms. My eyes only have so much time. I hold them below the sky that reaches out for everyone. All truth is the same. Disappearances are merely suggestions. We must go inside the beautiful bones that crack the clouds. Close your eyes, Samara. I want to know soon what it is I need to give back.

THE CANNIBALS NEXT DOOR

Their music is too loud, but I won't say anything. A promise tumbles from my mind as I close my book, whose sentences go awry. Their garbage unleashes itself, stops by all our houses, hopes for an invitation. I count the minutes as a strange language leaks from their windows. It's guttural and plans an escape. I hold up my eyes, see the cannibals' clothes waving in the dark or else the lack of them. They've gone wild, gnawing everything in sight, tossing all their belongings into a burning pile, dancing to the silence. Sex crawls up their walls and down their doors. They finally grow hazy, abandon their mouths, and leave for who-knows-where. Unfortunately, they always return.

DAMAGED

What was my food thinking? No vegetables. No fruit. A wet howl left in the throat. Arms tossed aside. There's too little between us. I know only so many songs to describe any situation, or the complications of every room, or what is expected of me.

I rest a pair of eyes upon my table. Can they see my good-luck woman undressed beside a lamp? I need her navigation, her social know-how, her clamoring for more. Some days she's a spear in my side. Other days her arms circle me like fish, and I nibble them in gratitude. She knows all my bad thoughts, and she holds each of them until they have become crooked paintings on a wall.

Objects, not people, become the place. I have ordinary pots and pans, chairs, spoons, forks, used every day. I breathe. Some days I'm too quiet. A spoon against a pot. A fork against a chair. Food in a pan. I just want to see how dinner will happen.

THE OTHERS WATCH A MOVIE

Small fish are airborne as the man asks directions. Where is the river? The smell of men and women surround him. The man bares his teeth as signs of life shake themselves, speak, move against a wall. The man goes round and round with the wind, although there is none.

Scenarios multiply like gods in front of his chair. There's too much noise and the man holds his hands over his ears, although no one around him is talking in that other language. The man lays down his clothes. He hungers for torn things shimmering across the screen, but when he reaches for them, finds only a veil. He searches for eyes. His hands try but air laughs at him. The man touches the light and becomes the light. He raises the veil and all the others flee.

SKIN LESSON WITH CLOUDS

The man holds everything inside. Someone tears a hole in the sky and more men fall out like clouds. In his dream he throws spears. Fibulas are visible, then disappear. Blood drips. People pay for the privilege.

There is no place to go without assembling. No one needs instructions. He hears ambulances, feels the pinch of medicine. Where is this life? Samara? He watches sky at his window, the well-intentioned clouds. People come and go. Words in another language hold him by the throat, shaking him. The man wishes to be a better person, named Bruce. Someone brings a white coffin and someone else a mirror. The man's face is a secret although Bruce sees through everything.

SELF-HELP

Tick-tock offered the unappetizing heart. The man wasn't sure what he should learn from blood arcing in air. *You're fine,* he was told again and again. He believed he wasn't because the people in bone-white spoke in riddles. Their walls were covered in whiter clouds that grew closer.

He watched the old woman sleeping next to him reveal her body's organisms spreading loosely around the world. *No wonder,* the man thought.

There was so much to be done. Some days the body could be fixed, but the parts of people that disappeared were the best parts. They didn't always return. Those white clouds had enormous appetites.

DARKER THAN I REMEMBER

1

My body was right all along, offering incremental disasters.

Cannibals laughed in the white room.

I was fond of being lit up repeatedly. Flowers couldn't help moving closer, needing to find their own diversions.

2

A language no one admitted using sprouted plastic chairs and sullen beds. Darkness was between us. I didn't want to pick the sudden door. Too much left me counting my toes and fingers.

My body was different, as usual.

3

My limbs couldn't be taught consolation. A mirror tucked all my blood in. I remembered instructions for disappearing, new clothes, a tired mustache, shiny shoes, a bus ticket.

Darkness stacked my body up (unseen and frayed). No matter what was done to it, it resembled a boy held
inside a bottle,
inside a forest,
inside calamity.

No one was left to apologize.

THEIR TINY JARS

The face was waiting at a blind window behind a sad, deluded tree, among the many. A stone whispered. Maybe it was the end of remembering how others filled the man's thoughts. The face saw through overwrought features to people's limbs and their tiny jars to the hidden rooms they stepped away from. In their houses they huddled together. None of them understood this.

He wasn't afraid, exactly. The face was beautiful, resembling birds that had already flown away, although he tried not to look at it.

He wasn't ashamed exactly. Although the face hovered like a balloon.

He clicked his teeth at the world, waiting for what would happen next, hoping he hadn't already swallowed these people's god.

FRAGMENTS OF THE SELF-CONTAINED MAN'S DIARY

Tuesday
I wanted another since they kept on coming. Body on top of body, saying something important. Fields were full of them and they only stopped for good news or money. They wanted to know who did what to whom. Inside out, they were nothing but air.

I was watching the future pass by helpless scenery, others, weather, my ideas. I was setting up my fetishes in a row, then knocking them down for fun. I was never good with people because they needed too much. My greatest moment? Plugging a leak.

Thursday
The Place said I wasn't where I was supposed to be. They said there'd be no food to bark at me. I had a conversation with the moon, misplaced my spoon, lifted my hands. I had a family who couldn't be ignored. Remembering all the accidents, I went to the nearest landscape, waited for something to shatter.

Friday
The person I was supposed to be refused to leave, face caught in angles of another, red and moving, with my mouth. I didn't know what door to use or what kept the house together.

I didn't like the woman they had given me. She told bad stories, then more bad stories. Her body, a box that echoed, whispered and I tried not to listen.

Sunday
I climbed back into my face so I could visit another. Birds flew across rivers, gods poked everything with their long sticks, windows described my eyes. The sun knew me better than I did. What the other said grew loud. I begged the sun to place someone else in this empty world so I could return to mine.

Night held everything in place. I couldn't see the neighbors, their delicious pets, mirrors with their answers, skin covering a bumpy heart. My hands were busy, blindly reaching. Everything trembled, stayed put, darkness filling in.

Monday
One more past arrived. I returned. Body on top of body, saying welcome.

LAST HOURS

Tell them nothing was wasted since the meat had nothing to say except how it remembered fields, grass, one version of itself. I was blinded by the inside of everything in the room. My distant relatives swung from hooks without touching. Moon withdrew, having already filled my mind. A faucet dripped.

Night and I glimpsed the world behind this world, which meant seeing the end before the beginning and meat as its own exchange.

Pressing bodies sloshed at air, quivered below the moon. I wanted to float. Everything was moving, nothing was alive. A door slammed.

Where else could I speak to those I ate? (There was no blood involved, in case anyone asked.)

I didn't know where to start. I sat in a human chair, used human eyes.

CANNIBALS AMONG US

I grow closer to them without knowing. A beautiful woman around the corner is making a killing. We wave talismans at one another. Mine are plastic. This strange, yellow-haired woman holds a bone, an egg, tiny stars knocked out of the night sky. She wants to sell them. She says she was born under a red moon and was spit out by the sea. She had to run through the forest. She tells me that I can't find what I'm looking for, which is everything. My language confuses her. *How much?* I ask. But she shakes her head, uproots her thoughts, spreads her wares on the ground. Her teeth are sharp and her hands crawl everywhere. Her long dress moves too close to me and I move away. *My pockets are empty of music,* she says, unsure. I'm in the shadows. Her striped shirt flaps under her straw hair. *Taste me,* she says, maybe meaning something else. And then I do. I do.

LAURIE BLAUNER is the author of six books of poetry, including, most recently, *Wrong*. A poetry chapbook called *Figments (& other occurrences)* was published in 2013 by dancing girl press. She also is the author of three novels from Black Heron Press—*The Bohemians, Infinite Kindness,* and *Somebody*. A novella was published in 2011 by Main Street Rag. She has received a National Endowment of the Arts Fellowship as well as Seattle Arts Commission, King County Arts Commission, 4Culture, and Artist Trust grants and awards. Her M.F.A. is from the University of Montana. She was a resident at Centrum in Washington state and was in the Jack Straw Writers Program in 2007. Her work has appeared in *The New Republic, The Nation, The Georgia Review, American Poetry Review, Poetry, Slate, Mississippi Review,* and many other magazines. She lives in Seattle.

TITLES FROM
WHAT BOOKS PRESS

POETRY

Molly Bendall & Gail Wronsky, *Bling & Fringe (The L.A. Poems)*

Laurie Blauner, *It Looks Worse Than I Am*

Kevin Cantwell, *One of Those Russian Novels*

Ramón García, *Other Countries*

Karen Kevorkian, *Lizard Dream*

Patty Seyburn, *Perfecta*

Judith Taylor, *Sex Libris*

Lynne Thompson, *Start with a Small Guitar*

Gail Wronsky, *So Quick Bright Things*
BILINGUAL, SPANISH TRANSLATED BY ALICIA PARTNOY

ART

Gronk, *A Giant Claw*
BILINGUAL, SPANISH

Chuck Rosenthal, Gail Wronsky, & Gronk,
Tomorrow You'll Be One of Us: Sci Fi Poems

PROSE

Rebbecca Brown, *They Become Her*

François Camoin, *April, May, and So On*

A.W. DeAnnuntis, *Master Siger's Dream*

A.W. DeAnnuntis, *The Final Death of Rock and Roll and Other Stories*

A.W. DeAnnuntis, *The Mermaid at the Americana Arms Motel*

Katharine Haake, *The Origin of Stars and Other Stories*

Katharine Haake, *The Time of Quarantine*

Mona Houghton, *Frottage & Even As We Speak: Two Novellas*

Rod Val Moore, *Brittle Star*

Chuck Rosenthal, *Are We Not There Yet? Travels in Nepal, North India, and Bhutan*

Chuck Rosenthal, *Coyote O'Donohughe's History of Texas*

Chuck Rosenthal, *West of Eden: A Life in 21st Century Los Angeles*

LOS ANGELES

What Books Press books may be ordered from:
SPDBOOKS.ORG | ORDERS@SPDBOOKS.ORG | (800) 869 7553 | AMAZON.COM

Visit our website at
WHATBOOKSPRESS.COM

www.ingramcontent.com/pod-product-compliance
Lightning Source LLC
Chambersburg PA
CBHW020059020526
44112CB00031B/492